# THE MIRACLE OF

# MEDITATION ORACLE

# GUIDEBOOK

ISBN: 978-1-954642-22-5

Emergence Education
P.O. Box 63767
Philadelphia, PA 19147
EmergenceEducation.com

Cover and interior design by Sophie Peirce
Original cover art and illustrations by Silvia Rodrigues

Printed in the United States of America.

# *The*
# MIRACLE *of*
# MEDITATION
# *ORACLE*
## GUIDEBOOK

## JEFF CARREIRA

EMERGENCE EDUCATION

*Philadelphia, Pennsylvannia*

# CONTENTS

Advocating *for a* New Way *of* Knowing. . . . . . . . . . . 1

*The* Miracle *of* Meditation . . . . . . . . . . . . . . . . . 9

Intuition, Science, *and* Alternative Forms *of* Knowing . 19

Divination, Imagination *and* Hermeneutics. . . . . . . . 33

Using *The* Miracle *of* Meditation *Oracle* . . . . . . . . . . 47

Thank You . . . . . . . . . . . . . . . . . . . . . . . . . . . 59

Selected Bibliography . . . . . . . . . . . . . . . . . . . . . .61

About the Author . . . . . . . . . . . . . . . . . . . . . . . .63

IF THIS WERE A DREAM, IT WOULD
ALL FEEL EXACTLY THE SAME. SO,
HOW DO YOU KNOW IT'S NOT A DREAM?

# ADVOCATING
## *for a* NEW WAY *of* KNOWING

*In order to open to the wisdom that is available through oracle cards we must transcend the natural skepticism and doubts of the modern age.*

*T*HANK YOU FOR USING The Miracle of Meditation Oracle and for downloading this guidebook. This is not a typical guidebook because I am writing it with four different intentions in mind. In this brief introduction I will explain what this book is intended for so that you can decide which parts of it you feel drawn to use.

## The First Three Intentions for this Book

1. For everyone who purchased the Miracle of Meditation Oracle, it provides some background information about this deck and how to make the best use of it. Chapters one and four are most relevant to this aim.

2. For people who are not familiar with oracle decks, it provides some background information on the history of divination and how it works. Chapter three focuses on this.

3. For people who are already familiar with oracle decks and divination, it offers an exploration of why the intuitive way of knowing is not generally accepted in our society. Chapter two focuses on this.

## The Fourth Intention for this Book

I imagine that the vast majority of people who would buy the Miracle of Meditation Oracle are already familiar with divination as a powerful way of gaining deep wisdom from a mysterious source. I don't need to explain anything to you, but I want to anyway. Why? Because I want to support you to be an even stronger advocate for the alternative way of knowing that the use of oracle cards represents.

As I said, I'm confident that you are familiar with oracle cards and how they give you access to secret realms of knowledge. I am also certain that you are aware that this way of knowing is not generally accepted in our culture. Often the other people in our lives find it difficult to understand why we would make important decisions based on messages received from random cards, but we know that there is more going on than our culture is willing to accept and understand.

A few months ago I had a tarot reading because I was feeling that something was opening up in my life and I wanted to ask for guidance about how to align with what was possible in the most optimal way.

The cards told me that I needed to spend time near the ocean and give myself space to contemplate what was coming.

I live in Philadelphia, but I had access to a house in Florida. I flew down to Florida as soon as I could and spent ten days contemplating near the ocean.

Many things have changed in my life in the months after I visited Florida. It would be hard to directly connect them to those ten days. Many people would certainly say that it was all coincidence, but I know there was a connection.

Now I want to share a fourth intention that I have in writing this book. I want to invite you to act as an Artist of Possibility and advocate for the value of this different way of knowing in the world.

I use the phrase Artists of Possibility for people who are awake to different possibilities for human life and who are bringing those possibilities into manifestation in their lives. Artists of Possibility are advocates for new ways of being. I think you are one of these and I want to support you in that.

In this little book you find an exploration about the current state of consciousness in the western world and why the new consciousness that we are awake to is not accepted and often rejected. I hope that what I share about how this situation came about will help you be an even stronger advocate for a different way of understanding reality. That is why I included it in this book.

Sincerely,

*Jeff Carreira*

CONTENTMENT *and* RELAXATION
ARE THE SAME THING, IF YOU WANT TO BE
CONTENT ALL YOU HAVE TO DO IS RELAX.

# *The* MIRACLE *of* MEDITATION

*You are already awake and free*
*even if you don't think you are.*

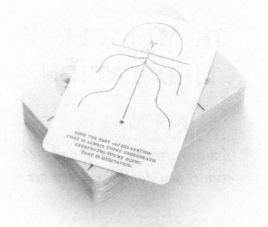

FIND THE REST and RELAXATION
THAT IS ALWAYS THERE UNDERNEATH
EVERYTHING YOU'RE DOING.
THAT IS MEDITATION.

𝒥'M BEST KNOWN AS a teacher of meditation and spiritual awakening. I've been guiding people through their spiritual journey for over twenty years and during that time the core of what I've taught has never changed. I teach the miracle of meditation, which is the discovery that there is a place inside yourself that is and always has been, peacefully at ease, content, and deeply receptive, no matter what your mind happens to be doing. Or to put it another way: you are already awake and free even if you don't think you are.

Generally speaking the miracle of meditation is discovered in two stages. The first stage is attainment and the second is realization.

When I teach meditation I teach it as the art of conscious contentment. That means the only thing I ask people to do is sit still, be relaxed and be content with whatever experience they happen to be having. It is a simple practice of choosing to be content right now no matter what is happening.

A person attains the first level of mastery when they develop a habit of being content that is stronger than their previous habit of being discontent and unsatisfied. Most of us come to meditation because we are unhappy. We find that the challenges we face in life consume us and we live in a mildly, or maybe deeply anxious state. We come to meditation to calm down and reduce our level of stress.

Through diligent practice we can learn to be consciously content in any circumstance, and if we practice long enough and hard enough, this can become our habitual way of being, so that no matter what is happening in our life we will tend to see it from a place that is calm, peaceful and free. This is the level of attainment.

Beyond attainment there is another level of awakening; the level of realization. There comes a point for the lucky spiritual seeker when they have a realization from which there is no return. This depth of realization is known by terms such as satori, awakening and enlightenment.

The realization I'm speaking about is the direct perception and recognition of the source of your own awareness. It is when you see for yourself that there has always been a part of you that is peaceful and free. That part of you is the awareness that is aware behind all of your experience. It is the pure consciousness called turiya in the Hindu tradition.

It is who you are before you know anything else. Recognizing this as the source of who you are is the level of realization.

At the level of realization we discover a deep source of awareness inside us and recognize it to be our True Self. This is the great realization that many of the world's enlightenment traditions are aiming towards. This is not a realization that comes by way of practice, it comes as a result of a profound spontaneous insight. This reality altering insight is always a gift of grace, an accident you might say. There is a famous phrase attributed to various sources that says in essence, "Enlightenment is an accident, but spiritual practice makes you accident prone."

Disciplined spiritual practice is certainly an important way to pursue the possibility of realization, but it is not the only way. Along with practices like meditation, many spiritual traditions use contemplation as a vehicle for transformation. Contemplating the often paradoxical insights that are revealed and articulated by those who have experienced awakening is a time-honored practice of enlightenment.

The cards in this deck can best be understood as part of the tradition of enlightened contemplation and especially what is often called *pointing out exercises* in the Buddhist tradition. A pointing out exercise offers a view of life from an enlightened point of view. These are often shared as statements of fact that are usually counter-intuitive because they stand in direct contrast to the way we've been taught to understand ourselves and the world.

The messages printed on each card of the tarot of The Miracle of Meditation Oracle can be thought of as pointing out exercises, and we make the best use of them by contemplating them until we begin to see the world differently.

As an example you will find a card in this deck that says:

**IMAGINE A PIECE** *of* **PAPER THAT IS BLACK ON ONE HALF** *and* **WHTE ON THE OTHER. THERE APPEARS TO BE A LINE SEPARATING THE TWO TWO HALVES, BUT THERE IS NO LINE. THERE IS JUST A BLACK SIDE** *of* **THE PAGE** *and* **A WHITE SIDE. THE LINE THAT SEPARATES THE TWO HALVES IS AN ILLUSION. IT DOESN'T EXIST. YOU ARE THE LINE THAT SEPARATES THE SPIRITUAL FROM THE MATERIAL.**

This statement is offering a different under-standing of who and what you are. You have been taught to see yourself as a person, an organism in a physical body. This statement is offering you a different perspective. You are not a person, you are the illusionary line that separates the spiritual from the material. On one side of you is the inner invisible world of spirit, on the other side is the physical world and all of the visible feelings of the mind and body. You are the line that separates the two. The line does not exist. You do not exist. If you think about this statement deeply enough it has the power to shift your consciousness into a radically different experience of yourself.

Another part of the contemplative tradition is the Zen koan. A koan is a paradoxical statement, usually in the form of a nonsensical and seemingly unanswerable question like, what is the sound of one hand clapping? or, does a falling tree make a sound if there is no one there to hear it? These questions have the power to cross wire the mental circuitry of the way we have been taught to think. The goal of a koan is not to come to a correct answer, but to come to an understanding beyond any answer. You will find that some of the cards in this deck contain koan-like questions. For example:

## WHO *are* YOU WHEN YOU FORGET YOURSELF?

This question asks you to go beyond any ideas you might hold about yourself and contemplate who you are beyond any self-concept.

This oracle card deck was designed to offer contemplations that have the power to shift your consciousness into a radically different experience of reality. There are many ways that the cards can be used as part of your spiritual journey, and as an aid to navigating through the challenges and complexities of life. We will discuss some of the ways these cards can be used in chapter four, but first there are a few more things to consider about how and why they work.

WHEN YOU DISCOVER THAT YOU CAN
BE AT PEACE NO MATTER WHAT
YOUR MIND IS DOING, YOU HAVE FOUND
THE CORE *of* YOUR BEING.

# INTUITION, SCIENCE, *and* ALTERNATIVE FORMS *of* KNOWING

*We know much more than we think we do
and we can do much more
than we think we can.*

$\mathcal{A}$ FASCINATING THING HAPPENED to me once that left me profoundly open to what I might be capable of as a human being. I had a friend who was a yoga teacher and she had invited me to do a private yoga session with her at her studio. I went and we slowly went through a beautiful sequence of flowing yoga asanas.

When the sequence was complete, my friend instructed me to lie down in the reclined pose known as savasana. The final pose of a yoga sequence involves lying still on your back with your arms outstretched by your sides. As I entered the savasana pose I found that my lower back was in tremendous pain. The pain was so acute that I was not able to lie flat on the floor. Instead I had to arch my back upward slightly in order to manage the pain. I had never experienced this before and I wondered if I had somehow injured myself, although given how gentle the yoga sequence was that seemed unlikely.

After a few uncomfortable minutes, my friend called for an end to the session and as we slowly made our ways to a seated position on the floor she told me that the session had been amazing for her. She told me that she had injured her back many years ago and in yoga she can never lie down comfortably in savasana. In fact, she told me, she always has to arch her back slightly just to be able to manage the pain.

*"Argue for your limitations and, sure enough, they're yours."*

~ Richard Bach

I was amazed. I told her about my experience. How had her pain transferred to my body? Neither of us knew. I hadn't known anything about her bad back and I certainly wasn't trying to do anything, and yet something had happened. I am using this story to make the point that we know much more than we think we do and we can do much more than we think we can. If we believe that there are things we cannot know and cannot do, we can be sure that we will not be able to know or do them. If we open to the truth that we don't know what we are ultimately capable of, then we have no idea what we can know or do.

In his book *The Flip,* my friend and colleague Jeffrey J. Kripal speaks about a shift in consciousness that flips a person into a completely different experience of reality. He calls people who undergo this transformation, flipped. A flipped individual has experienced something extraordinary, usually in the form of knowing something they should not be able to know or doing something they should not be able to do, and that experience has left them certain that reality is much stranger than they ever imagined and they have no idea what the limits of their own capacities are. If you are drawn to an oracle deck like this, I am sure that you are already flipped, but if you don't see yourself that way, I hope to convince you otherwise before you have finished reading this book.

This book is meant as a guide for using the oracle deck and the first thing to know is that an oracle deck is generally a set of cards each containing a word or phrase, and an image. The cards are meant to be used as seeds for contemplation, but the contemplation that they are meant to ignite is not deductive or analytic. As with the Zen koans we already mentioned, they are not puzzles to be solved. They are objects of contemplation meant to give you access to a storehouse of knowledge that lies beyond your normal rational thinking.

The primary justification for the use of oracle cards is the fact that there is wisdom that we have access to, but cannot reach with our normal ways of thinking. We gain access to this hidden wisdom through intuitive revelation, bursts of spontaneous insight that just appear to us without any logical precedent. It is not knowledge that we come to, it is knowledge given to us from an unknown source.

In order to open to the wisdom that is available through oracle cards we must transcend the natural skepticism and doubts of the modern age. Our culture has developed an almost unshakeable confidence in the power of logical reason. We are trained to believe that we can understand and figure out everything. This part of our cultural heritage will find it difficult that a word or phrase and an image that exists on a randomly chosen card could possibly tell us anything of value. Any meaning we derive from such a method must be pure fantasy.

Ralph Waldo Emerson the great American mystic poet believed that all knowledge ultimately emerges out of intuition. This is an idea worth contemplating. Where did the ideas we currently believe in emerge from? Perhaps they were logically derived from earlier ideas, but where did those ideas come from? If we follow the trail of ideas backward, there must have been a time when the original seeds

of the ideas we hold as true today occurred to someone as spontaneous intuitions.

*The primary wisdom is intuition.*
*In that deep force, the last fact behind which*
*analysis cannot go,*
*all things find their origin. "*

- Ralph Waldo Emerson

Certainly there is valuable knowledge that we
attain through logical analysis, but we also have
intuitive access to spontaneous knowledge. Think
about an intuition that you've had. Where did that
knowledge come from? Was it valuable to you?

In the book *Divination and Human Nature*, Peter T. Struck reminds us that the wisdom of oracles
has been a recognized and respected part of Western culture since the times of ancient Greece. Plato
wrote extensively about divined wisdom which was
seen as wisdom derived from a surplus of knowledge
beyond the normal grasp of our minds. Divination
was considered to be an art that could be developed.
People regularly visited oracles, people who had access to knowledge beyond the mind, to solve prob-
lems and gain insight into complex matters. It was
accepted among the ancients that there was wisdom

that could be gained through an oracle or medium who was skilled in reading signs and symbols.

Aristotle, another towering figure from ancient Greece who figured prominently in the early development of the Western mind, wrote extensively on the predictive power of dreams. Struck explains that Aristotle, while denying that the predictive power of dreams was divine, also believed that their predictive power comes from a place beyond human control.

Every high school student in the Western world learns about Plato and Aristotle. We learn mainly about Plato's understanding of an ideal realm of mind where everything real exists, and we are taught that Aristotle formulated one of the earliest versions of the scientific method. Their understanding and interest in divination and forms of knowing beyond human control is not generally a part of what we learn, but it is part of the intellectual system that we inherited from the brilliance of ancient Greece whether we are taught about it or not.

Our current cultural climate is heavily influenced by modern scientific materialism with a strong bias favoring validation by objective proof rather than inner revelation and intuition. Those of us who were born into the modern world are likely to have a strong allergic reaction toward forms of knowing that feel magical and unscientific. These attitudes will need to be transcended in order to unleash your awareness from the constraints of the rational mind.

In his wonderful book *Lost Knowledge of the Imagination*, Gary Lachman explores a different way of knowing - a knowing of the imagination. He offers a brief history of the birth of modernism focusing on how it led to the triumph of one form of knowing - knowledge gained by deductive reasoning, over a different form of knowing - knowledge gained by inner revelations of the imagination.

The Christian church won the initial intellectual battles of the medieval ages. The rivals of the church were the many alternative reality systems of the pagan world. The word pagan as it was used in the early church had a distinctly negative character because part of the church's strategy was to paint alternative beliefs and ways of knowing as evil. Words like witchcraft, demonic and sorcery, all retain some tainting of a negative character. This can be seen as evidence of how successful the church's propaganda campaign was.

Of course the church did not have a problem with wisdom derived from mysterious sources; its own sacred wisdom after all was essentially divined by priests from an unknowable God. The church was not against divine sources of wisdom, it was simply consolidating its power as the soul arbiter of higher truths.

As the intellectual revolution of the enlightenment proceeded, the church found itself under attack. The objective experimental knowledge of science waged its own war against what it saw as the superstitious ways of the church. We live in a world that is dominated by the scientific way of knowing. In these times anything that is labeled as scientifically proven, means that there is visible evidence to verify it, and that means that it is really true. Intuitions, and inner revelations that are not supported by visible evidence are seen as dubious at best. This cultural bias exists in anyone of us who lives in the modern Western world. For all of the great advances and benefits of science, it is still only one form of knowing. It is wonderful for knowing some things, but not everything.

Since the times of ancient Greece, it has been accepted that there are times when a different kind of knowledge is required. There are things that our rational powers of mind cannot figure out. The ancients went to visit oracles who had a connection with an alternative storehouse of wisdom. This wisdom has always been known to be tricky. It often presents us with riddles, and it always requires interpretation, but from the depths of our intellectual history, it has always been a form of wisdom that people have appealed to.

When people today use tools of divination or seek the advice of someone who does, it is because they realize that there is wisdom that they don't have access to in the normal ways. The scientific age paints these alternative ways of knowing negatively. Today they are less frequently characterized as evil and more often as childish refuges for weak-minded individuals who can't think effectively for themselves. This leaves many of us cut off from an important source of knowing. We have been injected with intellectual antibodies that destroy the credibility of any source of knowing that is not rational, logical, and evidence based.

With this oracle deck, I hope to inspire you to reclaim the power of your deepest intuitions by providing a tool that can spur an alternative way of knowing and give you direct access to a tremendous source of wisdom.

YOU ARE NOT AN UNAWAKENED BEING
WHO OCCASSIONALLY WAKES UP. YOU ARE
A FULLY AWAKENED BEING WHO SPENDS
A LOT *of* TIME CONVINCED YOU ARE
LESS THAN THAT.

# DIVINATION, IMAGINATION *and* HERMENEUTICS

*Divination is the act of receiving knowledge from an unseen source.*

𝒯HE LAST CHAPTER ILLUMINATED some of our modern cultural biases that will tend to cut us off from discovering our higher powers of divination and imagination. We should be clear that the battle for the imagination was not entirely lost. The alternative way of knowing was never completely vanquished. It continues to thrive in our spiritual and creative impulses. In this chapter we will explore the wisdom of imagination and relate it to the mechanics of divination.

The Miracle of Meditation Oracle is a divination tool. Divination is the act of receiving knowledge from a divine source, and for our purposes it is best to use a broad definition of a divine source. If we think of it as anything resulting from an unseen source, we will avoid associating it with any particular spiritual or religious tradition. So, divination then is the act of receiving knowledge from an unseen source.

The most well known deck of divination cards is the tarot. The tarot was created in 15th century Italy and was used initially as a card game, the precursor to the modern game of bridge. In his book *The Tarot: History, Symbolism and Divination*, Robert M. Place tells us that it was a tarot deck designed and created in Marseilles, France that eventually came to the attention of 18th Century occultists and became the model for our modern tarot decks.

I first used a tarot deck many years ago. I was at the time embroiled in a spiritual crisis that revolved around a business venture I was planning to start. The person I was working with did not share my spiritual ideals and although I had never used a tarot deck or had a tarot reading before, I decided to consult the cards to ask about this partnership. I randomly picked three cards and read about what those cards represented.

I don't remember which cards I picked, but I remember what I felt they said to me. The first one told me that I was involved with something that would not end well and that I wasn't being honest about it with my community. The second one told me that I still had time to change the course I was on. The third one told me that I already knew all this, and I was going to ignore the advice of the cards and go ahead anyway.

My heart started pounding in my chest. The cards were completely accurate. I had known everything they had revealed, including that I was going to ignore it. I felt as if these cards, randomly chosen from a deck, had seen exactly what I was up to more clearly than I had.

I remember quickly burying the three cards in the deck, putting all the cards back in the box, and returning it to where I had found it. I didn't touch another tarot deck for over a decade. The venture did end badly.

From that day forward I had a healthy respect for the tarot and the divination arts in general. I was also aware that the cards themselves did not give me those messages, I had interpreted those meanings from the cards. The cards themselves could be interpreted in many ways, but I seemed to know beyond doubt exactly the meaning that was meant for me.

Divination is not simply a passive reading of signs, it is an active interpretation of them. The messages in an oracle deck can be interpreted in many different ways, but if you are open to the wisdom they contain you will discover that they speak very specifically to you.

The art of divination is closely associated with the mysterious figure of Hermes Trismegistus. Hermes is not a well known name in the world today, but throughout the ancient world and into the Renaissance of 15th and 16th century Europe, he was a towering intellectual figure. The popular phrase "as above, so below" comes to us from the Hermetic text called *The Emerald Tablet* and it is a central tenet in the philosophy of Hermes.

Who is Hermes Trismegistus? I can refer you to no better source than Gary Lachman's *The Quest for Hermes Trismegistus: From Ancient Egypt to the Modern World*. In brief, Hermes was an intellectual figure of the ancient world who is associated with the Egyptian god Thoth and the Greek god Hermes, who is in turn associated with the Roman god Mercury.

The god Hermes was the messenger god with winged feet who would fly to the heavens to bring back words from the gods. This image characterizes Hermes, Hermetic philosophy and the practice of hermeneutics that we will discuss shortly. Central to Hermes and his philosophy is the idea of correspondence. Everything on Earth corresponds to something in the divine realms of the heavens - as above, so below.

Hermetic philosophy is central to the Western esoteric tradition of hidden, or secret, knowledge. *The Emerald Tablet* is considered to be a work in the Hermetic tradition and is a primary early text of alchemy. The ideas of Hermes are also central to the tarot, the medieval divination deck of cards which inspired oracle decks like the one we are exploring here.

In modern times Hermes is most actively alive in the discipline that carries his namesake, hermeneutics. Hermeneutics is the discipline of interpreting sacred texts and it is especially associated with the interpretation of the bible. If we take the term in a more general way it is the interpretation of any sign or symbol.

The world in the Hermetic tradition is a world of signs and symbols that point to things in the higher realms, but the corresponding higher meaning of the signs and symbols of the world are not easily deciphered. Correct interpretation is an art that must be developed and that art is called *hermeneutics*.

Each card of The Miracle of Meditation Oracle contains a phrase or sentence. The messages you find on the cards are poetic because their meaning is ambiguous and needs to be interpreted. The messages are generally simple to understand, but their exact meaning must be determined for oneself. As an example one of the cards instructs:

**TO HEAR LIFE'S GUIDANCE YOU MUST LISTEN WITH YOUR HEART.**
*Can you do that?*

On the surface the meaning seems clear and un-ambiguous, but upon deeper reflection we realize that this short statement contains two central metaphors that are open to interpretation.

The first is "life's guidance." What is life's guidance? We may have an immediate sense that we know what this is, but it would be beneficial for us to open to the possibility that we don't know and be receptive to discovering that there is more to life's guidance than we had imagined.

Similarly there is the metaphor of "listen with your heart." Again we might assume we already know what this means, but perhaps we don't. If we reflect on the phrase perhaps it will reveal a way of listening that we have never considered.

In the final chapter we will go into more detail about how to work with the messages on these cards, but for now it is enough to realize that the required art of interpretation is part of the time-honored discipline of hermeneutics. It is a way of looking beyond the words to discover the deeper, hidden meaning that they are revealing to you.

In the last chapter we looked briefly at how first the church and then science cast aspersions on all forms of esoteric knowledge, but in a broader sense that derition extended more broadly to the realm of the imagination in general.

The Age of Enlightenment championed the knowing of rational logic and visible evidence and spurred the counter-revolutionary movement of Romanticism. The romantic poets feared a scientific age in which the treasure and power of the human creative imagination would be lost.

The poet Samuel Taylor Coleridge wrote about the willing suspension of disbelief. Essentially he is referring to our ability to accept the seemingly impossible as possible. In order to engage with an oracle deck we must practice the willing suspension of disbelief. We must allow ourselves to be vulnerable to the possibility that cards randomly chosen might contain messages for us that apply to our current circumstances and offer wisdom that we would not otherwise have access to.

This challenges the very strong inclination of the modern world to separate fact from fiction. Facts are truths, fiction is made up. The wisdom we divine from a tarot deck or oracle card in the modern world looks like a form of fiction because in the modern world there is a sharp line that separates unambiguous evidence of fact from ambiguous words of fiction. Facts are true, fiction is not. The imagination is relegated to the domain of fiction. It might create beautiful things, but it does not generate truth.

In books like *Lost Knowledge of the Imagination* and *The Flip*, a different understanding of imagination is offered. Perhaps the line between fact and fiction, between the concretely observable reality, and the fantasies of pure imagination, is not as distinct as we believe.

I was originally trained as an engineer, and I did not need to work in the field of science for long to realize that there is a very fuzzy line separating fact from fiction. Scientists make up theories all the time. The existence of evidence may be clear and unambiguous, but what that evidence means about reality seldom is. Scientific facts are almost always interpretive. When a scientific theory is proven wrong we see that it was a fiction created in the mind of a scientist.

For example, we were for a long time certain that gravity was a force, but a century ago Einstein showed us that the effects of gravity are caused by curves in space. Inevitably we will realize something else down the track that will conflict with this fact. The scientific inclinations in us will want to say that science is made up of facts, and the knowledge we derive from things like oracle cards is simply made up. I would not want to argue that the wisdom of divination is made up of facts. I would instead argue that all knowledge is simply made up.

My book, *Higher Self Expression: How to Become an Artist of Possibility*, explores the creative power of the mind, and how our imagination co-creates reality. In order to engage effectively with an oracle deck we must understand that we co-create reality. Our imaginative powers allow us to interpret events and circumstances. We then act on those interpretations and as we do they become our reality. When we do this collectively we create realities that we all live in together. We assume that because everyone is experiencing the same things as real, that they must be real, until something changes and we discover that it was an interpretation.

When you use this oracle deck you will be co-creating the meaning of the cards. Your imagination will feel into what is being shared and if you are open and receptive your imagination will extend beyond its normal boundaries to touch an invisible source of knowledge. The wisdom you receive will be an interpretation, not a fact, but you will discover that the wisdom that comes to you through your creative engagement with the card will offer insight that would never have come to you through deductive reasoning alone.

IF THIS WERE A DREAM, IT WOULD
ALL FEEL EXACTLY THE SAME. SO,
HOW DO YOU KNOW IT'S NOT A DREAM?

# USING
## *The* MIRACLE *of*
## MEDITATION
## *ORACLE*

*The magic is not in the cards,*
*and it is not in you,*
*it is in the interaction*
*between you and the cards.*

$\mathcal{N}$ow it is time to discuss how to use The Miracle of Meditation Oracle. While I was thinking about how I wanted to instruct you to use these cards I felt myself start to become self-conscious. A skeptical voice in my head told me that I couldn't just make up how to use these cards. They weren't like tarot after all. They were *just cards I created.*

I let myself experience this feeling of self-doubt and wonder about it. It occurred to me that this point of view would be common among many people. After all, who was I, or anyone else to create an oracle deck out of thin air and then determine how they should be used? Shouldn't a deck like this come from some divine source? Shouldn't the way to use them be part of the initial revelation?

This is where things get very interesting. My self-doubting mind seemed to make a distinction between the oracle deck I was creating vs. the tarot, as if the tarot had a legitimacy that my cards lacked. Of course the tarot was invented by someone too, and as we have already seen, originally it was meant to be used only as a game for entertainment. Were those original game manufacturers divinely inspired?

Of course we don't know today who designed the first tarot cards and perhaps they were inspired by a higher vision, and there is no doubt in my mind that over the centuries as the tarot has been used as a tool for divination by countless occultists it has been charged with power that built up over time. I felt that power when I first picked up the tarot and used it to understand the circumstances in my life. Any tarot reader will tell you that a tarot deck has a power in it.

I would maintain, however, that the power of the tarot, or of an oracle deck, is not in the cards, it's not in the messages on the cards, and it's not in the images that illustrate the messages. A tarot deck in the hands of someone who is not open to them, or doesn't understand them, will remain dormant. It is just a deck of cards to the uninitiated, but in the hands of someone who has some understanding of what they are and is at least minimally open to them, they become powerful.

The messages of The Miracle of Meditation Oracle have come out of my own deepest spiritual realizations. They were born out of twenty years of intense spiritual practice and all of the access to higher wisdom my practice has blessed me with. I did not write the messages on the day that I typed them, I received that wisdom over decades of dedicated spiritual work. I wrote the words on the cards, but the wisdom was given to me from a mysterious source of inspiration.

The images on the cards were intuitively designed by Silvia Satya. Silvia and I have worked together for years. I chose her for this project because I have experienced her access to the intuitive wisdom of higher realms. Silvia created the illustrations by feeling her way into the messages and then intuiting, or divining, the illustrations you see on the cards. Some are more literal, some more metaphorical. You should use these images with the same vulnerable receptive mind that you use to read the messages.

In *Higher Self Expression* I draw many parallels between the spiritual work of great mystics and the artistic works of creative geniuses. Your interpretation of the cards you pull out of the deck will be personal, only you can discover it. The deeper meaning will not be in the literal meaning of the phrase, or the literal meaning of the images. The true deeper meaning will arise out of your creative engagement with the cards. The magic is not in the cards, it is not in you, it is in the interaction between you and the cards.

## Reading the Cards

As we have been saying there is an art to reading oracle cards. You will be reading both the words and the illustrations. Both the words and the illustrations are symbolic forms meant to act as a bridge or doorway to deeper intuitive wisdom. You should not simply read the cards, or look at the images. You should follow the words and the images into places of understanding that open up beyond them.

When reading the phrase on a card I suggest starting with a single slow reading and then turning away from the words to see what understanding and associations arise in your mind. Once you begin to get a sense of the meaning that wants to arise in you, return to the card. Read the phrase again. Allow the intuitive meaning to formulate more fully.

Avoid the temptation to try to figure out the meaning of the cards. Don't engage with the messages analytically. They are not riddles or puzzles to figure out. Their literal meaning is simple and you should accept it at face value. The deeper meaning is not found by analyzing the messages, it is found by following them into the inner realm of your own imagination. Allow the messages to guide you on an inner journey of discovery.

I suggest you engage with the graphic images on the cards in the same way. The illustrations will speak to you in the language of symbols that will further unlock the power of your subconscious mind. When I asked Silvia about how people should relate to the illustrations, she suggested that when you first look at the image on the card you should watch for your first spontaneous hit of meaning. Then deepen your understanding by continuing to look at the illustrations to see what else you notice and what other spontaneous interpretations jump to mind. Trust your initial hit, but then build on it until you feel complete.

## Daily Contemplation

One way these cards can be used is as a focus for daily contemplation. Each day set aside thirty minutes for daily practice. Pull a card randomly and contemplate it in the way described above. When you feel complete with the contemplation, close your eyes and sit in silence for the remainder of the thirty minute practice session. When the session is complete, reread the card to see if any new insights strike you. You might want to add to this practice some time to write down any insights you have in a journal.

## Contemplation for Specific Challenges

You can also use the cards as an aid in navigating through specific life challenges. When something has arisen in your life that you don't know how to deal with, give yourself 30-minutes and bring to mind the situation that you are facing. If you have a specific question you want to have answered, bring that question to mind. Then choose a card to focus on and follow the instructions for daily contemplation described above. As you engage with the card, keep relating what comes to your attention with the challenge or question you are working with. Ask yourself questions like: What does the card tell you about the challenge you are facing? What ways are you being guided to see things differently? What actions are you being encouraged to take?

**30-Day Contemplation**

Another way these cards can be used is in the form of a 30-day contemplation. This use is perfect when you have larger life issues or spiritual challenges that you want to transcend. To engage with the cards in this way, start by pulling one card that represents the overarching contemplation in relation to whatever you are dealing with. Take that card and place it somewhere, where you will see it everyday. Then engage in a contemplation of the card as described above.

For the next 29-days you will draw a different card each day from the deck. Contemplate that card as described above, but as you do, also relate it to the first card you pulled that represents the over-arching theme of the month. Notice how the wisdom and insight generated in the daily card changes when it is seen in light of the monthly card. You will probably want to write about the insights you have each day in a journal.

At the end of 30-days contemplate all of the insights that you have accumulated. Ask yourself questions like: What do they tell you about the original challenge you were facing? What ways are you being guided to see things differently? What actions are you being encouraged to take?

**Discover Your Own Way**

The point we made earlier was that the magic of an oracle deck is in the interaction between you and the cards. As I thought through my self-doubt about inventing how to use this deck, I realized that not only can I come up with ways to use these cards, but you can too. Part of your engagement with the cards involves deciding how you want to use them. You can create your own way to use the cards. Maybe you have a partner or a group of friends you would like to work with. Perhaps you want to use them to create a context for a meditation or yoga session. Be creative. Feel into how you are being guided to use the cards and take the risk to try it.

# THANK YOU

*T*hank you for using The Miracle of Meditation Oracle. It has been a joy to create this deck and I hope you derive tremendously valuable insights from it.

If you found the wisdom shared on these cards compelling and you want to explore what I teach about meditation and awakening more deeply, please download my free *Secrets of Profound Meditation* program or read my book, *The Experience of Luminous Absorption.*

If you have any questions or comments you want to share, please feel free to email me at: jeff@jeffcarreira.com

# Selected Bibliography

Carreira, Jeff. *Higher Self Expression: How to Become an Artist of Possibility.* Emergence Education, 2021

Kripal, Jeffrey J. *The Flip: Epiphanies of Mind and the Future of Knowledge.* Bellevue Literary Press, 2019

Lachman, Gary, *Lost Knowledge of the Imagination.* Floris Books, 2017

Lachman, Gary. *The Quest for Hermes Trismegistus: From Ancient Egypt to the Modern World.* Floris Books, 2011

Struck, Peter T. *Divination and Human Nature: A Cognitive History of Intuition in Classical Antiquity.* Princeton University Press, 2016

# About the Author

**Jeff Carreira** is a mystical philosopher, meditation teacher, and the author of numerous books including: *The Miracle of Meditation, The Art of Conscious Contentment, Higher Self Expression*, and *The Path of Spiritual Breakthrough*. Jeff teaches extensively online and leads retreats throughout the world.

Made in the USA
Coppell, TX
04 June 2022

78479481R00042